Gray
Wolves

Victoria Blakemore

ISBN 978-0-9988243-0-7

Photo Credits:

Cover, olga_gl/AdobeStock; 3, derwerbepool/Pixabay; 5, ew-anc.AdobeStock; 7, raincarnation40/Pixabay; 9, quickshooting/AdobeStock; 10-11, tpsdave/Pixabay; 13, zsoravecz/Pixabay; 15, sipa/Pixabay; 17, colfelly/Pixabay; 19, Abian_Valido/Pixabay; 21, lancealot21us/Pixabay; 23, raincarnation40/Pixabay; 25, diapicard/Pixabay; 27, derwerbepool/Pixabay; 29, raincarnation40/Pixabay; 31, USA-Reiseblogger/Pixabay; 33, skeeze/Pixabay

Table of Contents

What Are Gray Wolves?

Gray wolves are large mammals that are members of the **Canidae** family. Dogs are also members of this family, so they are similar in many ways.

Gray wolves have a mix of gray, brown, black and white fur.

Size

Gray wolves can grow to be up to 6.5 feet long and weigh up to 145 pounds. Males are usually larger than females.

Physical Characteristics

Gray Wolves have thick coat that is made up of different layers of fur. Their fur helps to keep them warm.

The coloring of their fur also works as **camouflage** by helping them to blend in to the colors of the forest.

Their large front paws let them walk on snow without sinking in.

Habitat

Gray wolves are usually found in forests. Their thick coat of fur allows them to live in cold **climates**.

They are also able to **adapt** to living in grasslands, the tundra, and even deserts.

Gray wolves are also called **timber** wolves because they are found in forests.

Gray wolves are found in parts of North America, Europe, and Asia.

In the U.S., most gray wolves are in

Alaska, around the Great Lakes,

and in the Rocky Mountains.

Diet

Gray wolves are **carnivores**.

They eat animals such as elk,

caribou, moose, deer,

beavers, and rabbits.

They prefer to eat larger

animals and can eat up to

twenty pounds of meat at a

time.

Gray wolves have strong jaws that allow them to break up the bones of their prey.

Hunting

Wolves use their sense of hearing to help them find prey. Once they find prey, wolves usually work as a group to hunt. They often surround an animal from all sides and will give chase if it runs.

Wolves that hunt alone are not as likely to catch their prey.

Communication

Wolves use different sounds to communicate with each other. They may bark, whine, growl, or howl.

Wolf howls are like human fingerprints. Each wolf has a unique howl.

Scent

Wolves also use scent to communicate. Wolves often mark their **territory** with their scent. Other wolves can smell them and will know to stay away.

Wolves can also use their sense

of smell to find prey.

19

Movement

Gray wolves have been recorded running at speeds of 38 miles per hour.

Like dogs, they are able to swim. They swim to cross bodies of water and to keep their coats free of dirt and mud.

Wolves keep their coats clean because they need them to stay warm in the winter.

Pack Life

Gray wolves live in groups of up to twelve wolves. These groups are called packs. The pack is led by two wolves known as the alpha and the beta.

The alpha is a male wolf and the beta is female. They are in charge of the pack.

Wolf Pups

Wolves have a litter of up to seven pups. When they are first born, pups are blind and have thin fur.

They are born in a den, which could be a hollow log, cave, or burrow.

The pack works together to take care of the pups. They also teach them how to hunt.

Social Animals

Wolves are social animals, they spend all of their time with the pack. They travel, hunt, and play together.

When the pups have grown up, some may leave to start their own family. Others may stay with the pack.

Wolves are playful with their pack. They like to chase each other, play fight, and pounce on each other.

Population

In the wild, gray wolves usually live between seven and eight years.

On **preserves** that are protected from habitat destruction and hunting, they may live as long as sixteen years.

In the United States, the largest
population of gray wolves is in
Alaska.

Gray wolves are important to the ecosystem. They are known as a **keystone species**. Other species in their ecosystem need them. By hunting animals like deer and elk, wolves keep their populations from growing too large.

If there are too many deer or elk, other animal and plant populations can decline.

The leftovers that wolves leave behind after they are finished eating provide food for animals that **scavenge**.

Coyotes sometimes follow behind gray wolves to eat their leftovers. Animals like buzzards will also eat their leftover prey.

Coyotes are scavengers.
They often eat the leftovers
from gray wolves.

Glossary

Adapt: to change or adjust

Camouflage: an animal's way of hiding by blending in with the surroundings

Canidae: a family of animals that includes wolves, coyotes, dogs, and foxes

Carnivore: an animal that eats meat

Climate: the usual weather in a place

Keystone species: a species

that other animals in the

ecosystem depend on

Preserve: an area of land used

to protect plants and animals

Scavenge: search for food

Territory: an area of land that

an animal claims as its own

Timber: the wood of trees

About the Author

Victoria Blakemore is a first grade teacher in Southwest Florida with a passion for reading.

You can visit her at

www.elementaryexplorers.com

Also in This Series:

Gray Wolves	Sloths	Flamingos	Camels	Koalas	Honey Bees	Pandas
Pangolins	White-Tailed Deer	Orcas	Giraffes	Corn	Meerkats	Echidnas
Walruses	Raccoons	Bald Eagles	Apples	Arctic Foxes	Red Pandas	Cassowaries
Tigers	Ladybugs	Moose	Beluga Whales	Leopards	Elephants	Jellyfish
Binturongs	Lions	Dolphins	Reindeer	Hammerhead Sharks	Hippos	Pumpkins
Peafowl	Chameleons	Florida Panthers	Aye-Ayes	Black Bears	Cheetahs	Manatees
Gingerbread	Polar Bears	Hot Chocolate	Orangutans	Coyotes	Marshmallows	Strawberries

All titles by Victoria Blakemore

Also in This Series:

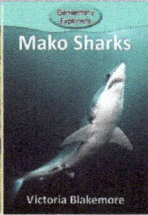

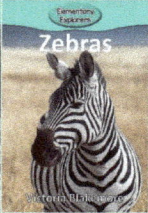

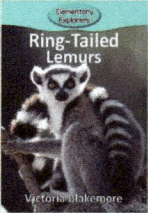

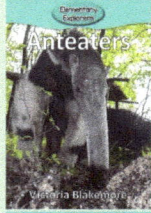

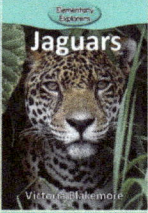

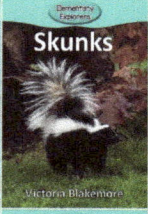

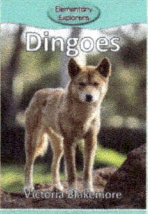

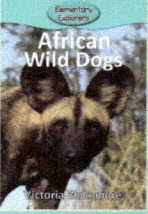

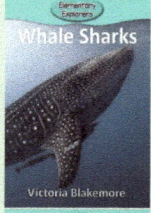

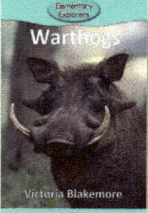

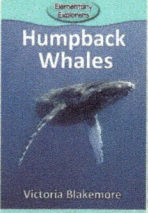

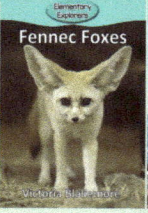

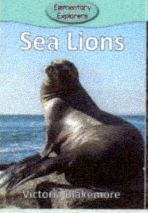

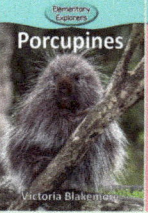

Elementary Explorers — Victoria Blakemore

Aardvarks	Mako Sharks	Alligators	Frogs	Hedgehogs	Brown Bears	Bongos
Sea Turtles	Quokkas	Muskrats	Zebras	Red Foxes	Ring-Tailed Lemurs	Platypuses
Anteaters	Kangaroos	Rhinos	Jaguars	Wombats	Capybaras	Gorillas
Cats	Skunks	Butterflies	Dingoes	Snow Leopards	African Wild Dogs	Penguins
Whale Sharks	Wolverines	Warthogs	Caracals	Badgers	Seals	Hummingbirds
Pikas	Humpback Whales	Pumas	Lemonade	Llamas	Tulips	Ostriches
Sunflowers	Fennec Foxes	Sea Lions	Squirrels	Roses	Porcupines	Ice Cream

www.ingramcontent.com/pod-product-compliance
Lightning Source LLC
Chambersburg PA
CBHW042249040426
42336CB00044B/3388